~~after the wound~~

Robin Ford

ARROWHEAD
PRESS

First published 2003 by:
Arrowhead Press
70 Clifton Road, Darlington,
Co. Durham, DL1 5DX
Tel: (01325) 260741

Typeset and printed by:
Arrowhead Press

Email: editor@arrowheadpress.co.uk
Website: http://www.arrowheadpress.co.uk

ISBN 0-9540913-6-1

 Arrowhead Press acknowledges the financial
assistance of Arts Council England, North East

Cover colour printing and finishing by
Firpress Ltd. Workington Cumbria

Contents

For the people who helped me break my ice,

Angela Buckland, Lydia Fulleylove,
Jaye Imrie, Shelley McAlister, Julie Sharp,
Joan Waddleton, Eddie Wainwright.

Injury

Call me Philoctetes
  it's good enough
I was where I should not be
  they said
doing foolish things
  they said
it wasn't much.

Something in my brain
  a bolt
  a shock
unzipped raw things
  stunned me –
not sure of anything
I fired up
  did
was caught   wounded
  fell.

It showed itself
  my wound
  my mouth
(what is the difference?)

then half-hidden
  cut dead
a walk through the hotel
in stiff silence –
a few half nods.

Consensus:
removal disposal
   expulsion
a rotten egg from a shocked ovary
that evacuation over
passage resealed
wound hid fast
   ingested.

Then to beautiful terrible here –
I saw them sail
owls   pussycats
happy after five minutes
they had done the right thing
   to abandon me
who was for so many years
a part of their triumphant days
now one whose name was shit on water.

He Wakes Abandoned

sea distant
not buoyant
beneath boat

strange light
new silence

(but as in a distant land
I seem to recognise)

someone
bring me water
here over here –

no bastard bothers

it is too quiet
no white sounds
of quotidian life

Serpents

which one did for me –

the serpent that thorns my guts
the heart-croucher snake
which coils about its brain-laid eggs

the one like avid bindweed
which corkscrews bones
in either leg

or the Amfortas snake
of wounded testicles –

did it crouch in that forbidden place
waiting

it sprang
struck
no cure likely
(prognosis poor)

even healing
would leave scars
stains

And He Questions

Hope   virtue   survival

what counts in a cave
where heat and cold
harsh calls of indifferent birds
and rival waves beat
through twenty four hour nights
till dawn dies immediate
in bloody sunset.

What relief   or reason
when my story
(all that I have)
leads only to an unmarked death
what hold?

It is as though I clutched at glass
when falling
my bones and hair
on rocks
torn as gulls
gale-beaten into cliffs.

Nothing –
no whisper
no heir nor any mark

I wish eternity to oblivion.

Gradualia

air even in apparent stillness
shivers chill

when a gale stings in from ocean
it is enemy armed

waters beneath gather
insinuate aches into my bruised bones

these are my perpetual pains

they me   I they

*

I have killed to keep
my vacuum and husk
in life

it is time to repay
in my own polluted currency

I cut my flesh
an existence lives in pain
but it is I who act here –
for these minutes
liberty shoots from a sharp shell

*

my home my hills –
memories are shed scales
I circle my island's shores
as if they were blind corridors

I will cut my blackened heart
to freedom
rip my dark paper
till blood shows the sun
I too have colour

*

in my hand a coral branch
sharp as razor wire
I plough my rough skin
till red mud seeps –
if you are there God
you shit
just watch this –

> *fucking little treacherous thought*
> *slug! spider! Inhibitor*
>
> *how quickly you scuttled in*
> *lodged like a virus*
> *I will never get you out*
>
> *I hear you bleat*
> *it is not the end*
> *you can live from within*
>
> *and a snigger*

you have beaten me

The Weight Of Expectancy

They said I had knowledge
    I had no knowledge

what they piled on me
bowed my spine

how did they dare
plant snake wisdom
in my very seed?

    I refused knowledge
    became beast and bore
    under burden of election

    when electric air flicked
    I could tap that
    make them laugh, spark them
    though power drained out of me
    vital essence turned air
    a little death of sorts

which led to dark flaccid times
I a forced plant
defences blunted
shadow shrunk
sleight of hand my last resource
life rung out
litter for the bin

I felt as they felt
    betrayed
thus for a short while
we were at-one

What Now?

As I walked along the beach
    today

I saw   you   was it

at a cavelet's mouth
first beyond reach   then out of sight

days here shuffle unoriginal and old
I count my knuckles a hundred times
arrange stones into words, flowers, sums
imitate birds
recall poems
revive tunes

I speak to absent crowds
move with the slow sway of branches –
sea is a wind-drone instrument
keening imbecilic sighs.

I will start an inward journey
to my unknown ocean
which lies further than a chain of caves

Voices

Human silence
many birds much sea
nothing startles or jolts
into pleased or hostile rebound

if a voice called
I no longer know whether
my heart would leap or sink

waves deep as gale blown lyres
now are language
speak to me in secret tongues –
my own voice I rarely hear
surprise myself sometimes
with coils of unformed soliloquy

I may catch a voice
like a near echo
words pass in wind
sparks from a blown bonfire
bright then nothing
just in reach as though
the excluding wound
uttered its own sounds
guttural   broken

Romantic

Some days sea licks sands
with soft roughness of an idle cat
tells itself stories
half-beliefs of nymphs and sirens
men and women
playing so far out from land
that blue turns black and gold.

I make sand pillows
clasp hands beneath head
think of those few I loved
if only for a single hurried night –
some beyond recall
only parts – smile smell word – remain
bright as eyes of birds
gorging ripe berries

but time and again it is a single face
which forms from vapour streams
into a brilliant cloud
I imagine one ancient kiss
brushes me then drifts to fall as showers
on a distant drought struck isle.

Recurrence

That dream again
which shakes me
to sour consciousness so many nights

only the sea's insistent rumble
lulls me back to sleep
once more to wake arms stretched
appalled by bile erupting in my throat.

When morning comes
(as it does so many times a night)
I wake to find companions gone –
they waited for pain and mania to exhaust
maybe slipped me pills or pushed oblivion
through my veins
then left me bare beneath a scrawny salt sick tree
which leant and shook in night freshets.

I wait for them to knock the door
drinking over   time called
but they have driven on elsewhere

other mornings I wake false
beside a bed companion of my form
who is not me and every blanket
crawls with life of woodland floors

no-one there in such fake dawns –
I cower in ceiling corners of unknown rooms
stick there – try camouflage
when true morning comes

no difference
same sea pushes waves of sour recall
over my spluttering mouth

it drowns me dark

Gap

If I see home again
it will have slipped
beyond my reach

I will pass familiar buildings
sit on a favourite seat which looks
seaward
        as here but not like here

saplings will be trees
animals grown tired and easy

I will have missed them
children most of all
will never catch
vital histories of small important things

there will be nothing reliable to read . . . .

but here sunlight slides across the red cliff
a tree leans just in balance
twigs spread amazed fingers
rocks take new colour from rain

at such times I live seconds
which are hours

I could claim revelations
but I think I enter my own light
step into my own round

recalls   lost experiences   past flames
these are my mysteries and my delights.

Reality And Image

If they abandoned me
were they my friends?
   They were.
If it exiled me
was it ever my land?
   It was.

Comradeship – a fine dangerous thing
wrong shoes wrong views = exclusion
disaster swift as whips at a false step
        was the snake born in me
        and not beneath my boot
it was not my wish

reasons they gave   reason after reason
enough to deafen them

after they had gone
survival harsh as sea hawk's talons
rejection scraped my open bone
wounds heal but are signed by scars
a crushing shame that I was caught in this

        but a type of grace when images fly
        in my mind-web
        stick there   shake all parts of it

        for days one thing overrides
        blocks in full eclipse
        then I am filled – say – with remembrance
        of a marble threshing floor
        beyond our farm – a circle unmoved by seasons
        nacreous in summer lapped with chaff and dust
        a burning gibbous moon

Worms Butterflies

I swam this morning
in nakedness which still troubles me
splashed water
watched my feet ripple
turn mackerel
dipped head under in ungainly handstands
felt salt-lines in my mouth
a clean sting in my wound

returned to shore
lay back felt so happy
so at-one
until that inner malicious mouth said
    why do you feel so good
    what reason have you to feel so good
silence falls to the enemy
but
also the voice invokes love

I think I learn
    I could pretend fire is friend
    rocks my protectors
    but will not fool myself
I take what is
more will come

Transformations

I watched dolphins a little way out
    time demons
leap element to element
some rose further
    one did not return to water
    became albatross
    disappeared to far ocean
then I knew time would link
I would find my land
meet myself   my secrets   my songs

and I knew them – my betrayers
thin-skinned as me
always near fearful boundaries
I might have joined their side – the crowd
that is – against the one or two
outsiders   aliens even
had I been in majority
suddenly a new voice leapt inside me
hard to recognise or place as mine
light blazed dimming sun
came from deep caves
burned inward and then out

world rang for one moment
like bells at start of earthquake
then steadied
radiance swelled and clasped my world
each crawling insect stunted plant
held in arms sprung from me
inadequate to grasp world's loveliness
which stretched and streamed

tiredness brushed me almost as a friendly nudge
not numinous but of a well filled working day
I slipped to sleep, gateway into refuge
and through that arch I saw a face beautiful
but ill-defined that shone and faded
a woman's face lit within
        I cannot describe it more

with a gift like gold I slept
random things – dust light took form
     clay on a wheel
     a rock packed in silk
     world in an egg
     the falling moment

the figure   feet of air
moves inward
thyme   rosemary

she siren/serpent
my dea ex machina
contrived with cunning

I spread-eagled by time demons
who have overcome the waves

she looks at me
        and beyond this I must not think now
face dissolves
projections on my mind's blank wall
holograms   shadow puppets
a dream of fair women
        I see:

Leonora
  Gretchen
    Lulu
      Hilde
        Melisande-Melusine
          Big-Foot Bertha
            Viola
              Albertine
                Laura
                  Yseult
                    Mnemosyne
in Botticellian dance

Dea Ex Machina or Dream Pantomime
or What You Will

Either (a) Philoctetes is overcome by intense slumber and thus, void of
consciousness, is transported back to his own homeland in the Real
World (a sneaky trick)

Or (b) the dream of fair women continues (Choose either or a version
of your own)

But if (b) she who comes sailing in
HMS HELIOS
introduces herself as
Commander Amy Bathos-Simpson
sent to bring the exile home
after certain crises of conscience
regret medical discovery
petitions from a few loyal friends
(not as highly regarded by him formerly
fool that he was as those who abandoned him)
and a bit of politicking over usefulness
pragmatism vincit omnes

CMDR. BATHOS-SIMPSON: (to herself) Good God, I thought men
like that shot themselves.
    (to PHILOCTETES) Come along then my man, I'm here to fetch
you, under orders, to effect your recovery. Your Country needs you
– well permits you – to return.
    (she calls the FAIR HOLOGRAM WOMEN) Fall in there women!
Sisters!   (but they don't respond)

CMDR. BATHOS-SIMPSON: I preferred it when I had to work with
Valkyries. Mr. Philo – you see before you a person dedicated to duty
and not personal pleasure – though when I am on leave I will admit to
enjoying being a voluntary bat warden.

It is my duty, I cannot say pleasure, to conduct you back to Home
and Beauty.
Kindly step into the landing craft and we will depart.

PHILOCTETES: Farewell my cave, nymphs of riverside and field
My island, my music of sea and rock and spray
(the craft casts off)
Even transports such as these
are manic moments not delight.
Have I gone mad again?

Return And Accusation

Neither you nor I expected this
I am he come back to you
who banished me *my friends*
because a wound   a blameless wound
stank   could not be admitted
to our town's fine houses or drift its tidy streets
an embarrassment impossible to ignore

that wound   putrid wound
mouth to me
filled with grave liquor   gut infection
cried offence   poor wounded putrid mouth
so your tight arses clenched closer still

my flesh turned wound
forced on you the ever propinquity of rot
feared as you are of flies and pus
which was good enough for me
this mouth *my truth* made you stink to yourselves
fixed as you were one step beyond me
you wasted no time with cure – no honey/oil/hyssop
as in your scriptures
                 my words spouted
                 terrified you who rowed off
                 more than siren songs
                 easy blocked by wax
                 your expertise
my words hatched blowfly maggots
in your bound and secret wounds –
they could have cleared your yellow slough
                 but puny front-room knowledge
                 hid truth – that grubs will cleanse
                 save despite disgust
you feared and thus despised   sought distance   blindness
I let maggots do their good work

see me here healed

It is I who gag at the stink of your hidden wounds
ulcers grown from tiny stings
sick in every skinfold under every stitch
all of them mouths to scream your souls out
I deafen to your howls of panic when you behold
wholeness and recovery approach.

Vox Pop

He's back now. I wouldn't wish him away, not back on that rock. What they did to him wasn't right but I have to say I'm rather disappointed in him – and that's on a good day. To be fair to myself I joined the campaign to free him and that was because he had been a decent kind before. It was definitely wrong to exile him or anyone like that. But he has changed which is not surprising, you can't warm to him. Abrupt. Moody – as if he's still on that island alone – even irritable, uncouth sometimes. There's plenty who are against him still. You can see why they put him off that ship.

*

I don't trust the bastard. Tell my kids to keep away. What does he look like dressed like that? And he's the sort they give houses to not decent local people who have worked hard all their lives

*

I think he suffered and I respect him – we have him round to supper every so often but it's hard going – he's no conversation except that island of his and I don't really think he's saying everything about that – holding things back. Best left alone.

*

Fucking loony. Muttering away. What's the fuss about? Says he's cured and we're sick. Send the bugger back.

*

I was indeed a member of the crew and I certainly took part in putting him ashore. I think it is very easy for those who were not there to be critical and I feel it is for them to say what they would have done in the circumstances. There are times when the greater good comes first. I make no apologies for that.

*

We are aware of public feeling. We will keep the situation under review.

So He Continues

I wander though each daily street
with my treasure I cannot look at
and must not reveal
protect it   hide it
never let it waste or leach away

I get odd looks
that's the price – OK by me
what I carry with me will neither die
nor fade
its elements crystal

I must hold my shining secrets
         whilst I live.

Acknowledgement

Two of the poems in this sequence, *Voices* and *Recurrence*, have been previously published in *Brando's Hat.*